JESSE JAMES

JESSE JAMES

Published by Creative Education, 123 South Broad Street, Mankato, Minnesota 56001
Creative Education is an imprint of The Creative Company
Design and Production by EvansDay Design

Photographs by Buffalo Bill Historical Center; Cody, Wyoming; Vincent Mercaldo Collection
(*P.71.2167*, cover, p. 2; *P.71.2175*, p. 8; *P.71.2157*, p.30), Corbis (Bettmann, John Springer Collection,
Bob Krist, Bob Rowan; Progressive Image, Galen Rowell, ML Sinibaldi, Joseph Sohm;
ChromoSohm, Inc.), Getty Images (Hulton Archive)

Library of Congress Cataloging-in-Publication Data
Frisch, Aaron. Jesse James / by Aaron Frisch.
p. cm. — (Legends of the West) Includes index.
ISBN 1-58341-338-3

1. James, Jesse, 1847-1882—Juvenile literature. 2. Outlaws—West (U.S.)—
Biography—Juvenile literature. 3. Frontier and pioneer life—West (U.S.)—Juvenile
literature. 4. West (U.S.)—History—1860-1890—Juvenile literature. 5. West (U.S.)—
Biography—Juvenile literature. I. Title. II. Legends of the West (Mankato, Minn.)
F594.J27F75 2004   364.15'52'092—dc22   2004058225 [B]

First edition

2 4 6 8 9 7 5 3 1

Cover and page 2 photograph: Jesse James as a teenaged Civil War guerrilla

—⋆≕ **Aaron Frisch** ≔⋆—

IN THE LATE 1850S, AMERICA WAS READY TO COME APART AT THE SEAMS.

As the nation neared its 100th birthday, it was divided into three distinct sections: the North, the South, and the untamed West. The North shouted for an end to slavery, "that peculiar institution," and the South fought to protect its slavery tradition. The terrible Civil War would soon begin.

In the woods, hills, and fields along the **Kansas-Missouri border,** however, the war had already begun. Settlers from both sides of the debate put down roots in these border states, where all three sections converged. Here, where one household was loyal to the Union and the next waved the Confederate flag, killing of a particularly savage sort started early.

It was from this bloody place and time that Jesse James rode into legend. Because of the shadowy nature of his short life, the tale of America's greatest outlaw is an inseparable combination of fact, myth, and speculation. He was a murderer and a thief to be sure. But many through history have also held him up as an avenger, hero, and even victim. No matter the labels attached to the name "Jesse James," his is a story for all time.

CHAPTER ONE

Under the Cloud of War

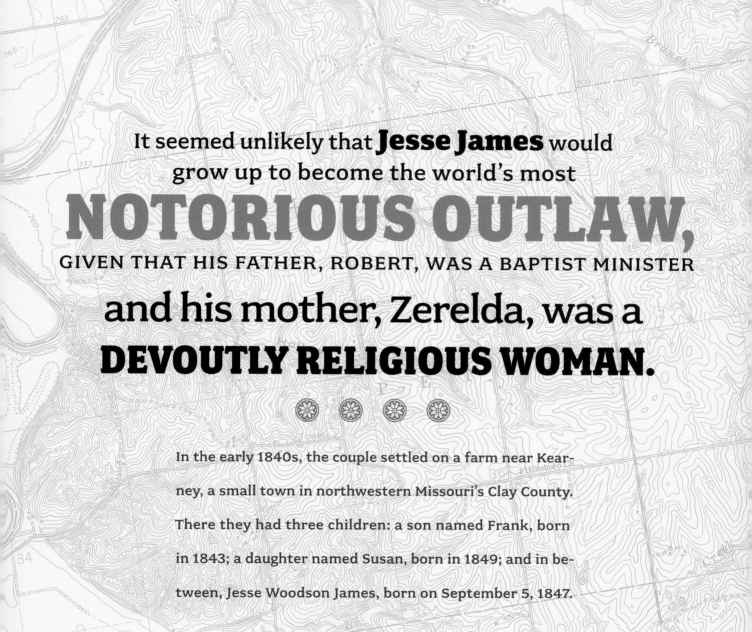

It seemed unlikely that **Jesse James** would grow up to become the world's most

NOTORIOUS OUTLAW,

GIVEN THAT HIS FATHER, ROBERT, WAS A BAPTIST MINISTER

and his mother, Zerelda, was a
DEVOUTLY RELIGIOUS WOMAN.

⚙ ⚙ ⚙ ⚙

In the early 1840s, the couple settled on a farm near Kearney, a small town in northwestern Missouri's Clay County. There they had three children: a son named Frank, born in 1843; a daughter named Susan, born in 1849; and in between, Jesse Woodson James, born on September 5, 1847.

Jesse James's mother, Zerelda, was a strong, opinionated woman who taught her boys to work hard very early in life.

Zerelda James was a tough woman who stood nearly six feet (1.8 m) tall, and both Jesse and Frank inherited her strong personality. When they were barely older than toddlers, the boys were already planting crops. Zerelda relied on them even more after their father—having traveled to California in hopes of striking gold—died of pneumonia in 1850. After a short-lived second marriage, Zerelda took a third husband in 1855: a country doctor and farmer named Reuben Samuel. Frank and Jesse got along well with the gentle doctor, who took them hunting and fishing but did little to stifle their rambunctious ways.

The Samuel farmstead prospered, becoming one of the largest in Clay County. This was due in part to the family's seven slaves, a possession that garnered them some unwanted attention. More abolitionist, or antislavery, settlers were filling up the border states of Missouri and Kansas, and a slave-owning farm was a target for fanatical abolitionists determined to stop slavery's westward expansion.

By the late 1850s, as Jesse approached his teens, the Kansas-Missouri border was a cauldron of violence. Unofficial soldiers called guerrillas banded together into militias that burned homesteads, looted towns, and murdered civilians and soldiers alike. Those who sided with the North, or Union, were known as "jayhawkers" or "redlegs." Guerrillas who fought for the South, or Confederacy, were called "bushwhackers." One of the most lawless and terrifying of the militias was a band of bushwhackers led by a former schoolteacher named William Quantrill and known as "Quantrill's Raiders."

William Quantrill

One of the most crucial influences on Jesse James's adolescence was William Quantrill. He was born in Ohio in 1837 but moved to Kansas at the age of 20. There he worked as a farmer and schoolteacher but fell into a life of gambling, horse rustling, and murder. Just before the Civil War, Quantrill emerged as the leader of a fierce guerrilla band, spurring his troops on with the Biblical cry "An eye for an eye and a tooth for a tooth!" Quantrill led his "raiders" through the dense forests and hollows of Missouri like ghosts in the night, launching brutal hit-and-run ambushes on Union troops and civilians loyal to the North. On August 21, 1863, Quantrill and up to 450 other guerrillas (including Frank James) descended on the town of Lawrence, Kansas, torching it and killing at least 200 men and boys. The Confederate hero met his end in May 1865, when he was surprised by Union guerrillas in Kentucky and shot off his horse. Thrown in jail with minimal medical attention, he died several weeks later.

When Confederate soldiers attacked South Carolina's Fort Sumter in April 1861, triggering the Civil War, Missouri officially remained loyal to the Union. Many Missourians, however, including the Jameses, sided with the Confederacy. To them, the Yankees, or Northerners, were tyrants looking to crush poor Southerners and erase their way of life. Zerelda, always fiercely proud of her boys, was never prouder than when 18-year-old Frank joined the bushwhackers. Although 13-year-old Jesse was equally eager to fight, the militia turned him away for being too young. So, as war engulfed the country, Jesse worked the Samuel farm.

As Union forces grew in Missouri, the Samuel farmstead came under suspicion as a bushwhacker hideout. In 1863, Union militiamen rode up to the farm looking for information. When Reuben and Jesse refused to talk, the guerrillas tortured the doctor by repeatedly hanging him from a tree, and they beat Jesse bloody with heavy ropes. Several weeks later, the militia returned and jailed the sharp-tongued Zerelda for more than a week.

Enraged, Jesse approached Quantrill's band again the next year; this time he was accepted. Despite his scrawny arms and fair features, the 16-year-old quickly earned respect with his fearlessness, hard riding, and skill as a spy. His toughness was illustrated when, shortly after joining the bushwhackers, he accidentally blew the tip of his left middle finger off while loading a pistol. His only reaction was to drop the offending weapon and yelp, "That's the dodd-dingus pistol I ever saw!" The nickname "Dingus" followed him from that day forward.

Jesse rode with some terrible men during the war. His best friend, Archie Clement, was a small, sadistic teenager who was an expert at taking scalps. William Quantrill was less a Southern patriot than a bloodthirsty killer, but his protégé—a dark-bearded sociopath named William "Bloody Bill" Anderson—was even worse. Anderson wept with fury in battle and was known to line up captured Union soldiers and shoot them in the forehead, one after the other. Jesse no doubt witnessed—and likely partook in—many such atrocities, as he rode under Anderson's command for much of his guerrilla career.

Although the bushwhackers were a thorn in the Union's side, the North proved too powerful. By 1865, Union general Ulysses S. Grant had the forces of Confederate general Robert E. Lee on the run. As the Union became confident of victory, it tried to snuff out Confederate guerrillas in the border states by destroying homesteads and chasing many rebellious families—including Jesse's—out of Missouri.

When the war came to an official end in early April 1865, President Abraham Lincoln offered amnesty, or a pardon, to all Confederate guerrillas if they would swear a formal oath ending hostility toward the North. By then Jesse was riding with a small band that included Frank and a hulking cousin named Cole Younger. Although the thought of turning in his guns to the hated Yankees pained him greatly, the desire to see his family again would soon drive Jesse toward Lexington, Missouri, to swear his oath.

Abraham Lincoln's assassination (which, strangely, resembled Jesse's death) helped make the post-Civil War years turbulent ones.

On April 14, a crazed Southern actor named John Wilkes Booth assassinated President Lincoln. The murder riled Union troops, some of whom met Jesse on May 15 as he rode toward them carrying a white flag of surrender. The soldiers opened fire, and a bullet to the chest knocked Jesse from his horse. As the bullets continued to fly, Jesse crawled into a ditch to hide. He remained on a creek bank for two days, delirious with fever, before a farmer found him.

Jesse had been shot in the chest the year before and had healed in six weeks. This time, though, his lung wound was so serious that he was sure he was going to die. Only with the gentle nursing of a pretty cousin named Zee Mimms was Jesse brought back to health. It was five months before he was strong enough to return to Clay County, where Reuben was rebuilding the farmstead.

With the war over, Jesse was left to consider his future. After more than two years of riding and killing, he had become a skilled fighter, and he could not bear the thought of walking behind a plow for a living. And then there was the bitterness that welled in him: the memories of his family's mistreatment at the hands of the Union militia, and the treachery that nearly killed him with a flag of surrender in his hand.

In late 1865, Frank James, Cole Younger, and other restless bushwhackers drifted into Clay County similarly in search of a future. Gradually a dark plan took shape. There was a way to both make a living and keep the war against the Yankees alive. They would hit the North where it hurt the most: in its bankbooks.

A Robber's Take

Over the course of their two dozen or so robberies, the James gang rode away with hundreds of thousands of dollars. It is often assumed, therefore, that Jesse lived a life free of financial worry, or even one of luxury. Visions of the outlaw living easy have been fostered over the years by legends that refuse to die. One long-lasting rumor holds that somewhere in the Ozark hills of Missouri and Arkansas are stashes of gold that the gang hid away while on the run and never came back for. In truth, Jesse lived a life of modest means and was nearly penniless when he died. Because he rode with a gang that frequently numbered eight or more, and because the loot was usually split evenly, no single take made him particularly rich. Although legend almost certainly distorts reality when it comes to Jesse's charitable donations, he was generous with fellow Confederates in need. The need for fast horses, numerous guns, and lodging while on the dodge had a way of depleting his bankroll as well.

CHAPTER TWO

The Making of a Legend

On a cold and blustery

JANUARY 13, 1866,

THE CASHIER AT THE

Clay County Savings Bank

IN LIBERTY, MISSOURI,

looked up as three men wearing long soldiers'

coats walked into the bank.

While two warmed themselves by the stove, the third

approached the counter and asked for change for

a $10 bill. An instant later, the cashier was looking

into the barrel of a Colt pistol. "I'd like all the money

in the bank," the man said evenly, "and quickly."

Minutes later, the three men exited the bank with cloth sacks holding nearly $60,000 in cash and bonds—an amount equal to almost $700,000 in today's money. They were joined by seven young men, including one the others called "Dingus," who had been watching street corners from their saddles. The gang fired furiously into the air as it left town, scattering citizens and killing one bystander. A posse, or temporary band of deputies, was hastily assembled but quickly lost the trail in the blowing snow. Missourians were shocked. It was the first time an American bank had been robbed in daylight during a time of peace. Shock turned to disbelief as three more Missouri banks were hit in the next 14 months.

Eyewitnesses to the robberies gave law officers the same description of one of the bandits. He was a good-looking young man of medium height and build, with small hands and piercing blue eyes that blinked more than normal. His manner was polite—as long as his commands were followed promptly. If they were not, his eyes turned to ice in an unspoken threat of violence. Combining this description with trails that led toward the Samuel farm, lawmen were soon looking for young Jesse James.

Attributing the crimes to Jesse was one thing. Catching him was quite another. The skills Jesse had developed during the war served him well, as he and his partners eluded their pursuers after robberies by moving along hidden forest trails, sleeping in caves one night and the barn loft of a Confederate farmer the next. If questioned, Jesse always claimed to have been working at the

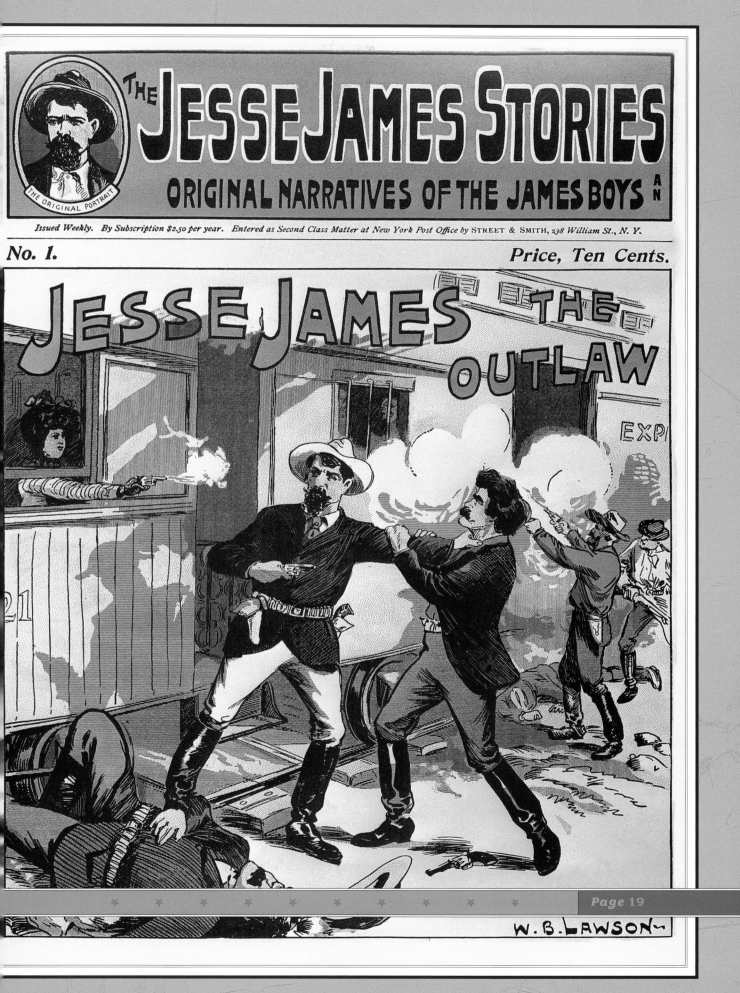

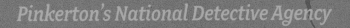

Pinkerton's National Detective Agency

The most competent and relentless opponent of Jesse and his fellow outlaws was Pinkerton's National Detective Agency. The agency was formed in 1850 and got its name and leadership from Allan Pinkerton, a former Chicago police detective. In its first decades of existence, the agency—which went by the motto "We Never Sleep"—earned renown for its protection of banks and railroads and was employed by the Union as a spy agency during the Civil War. The Pinkerton agency never slept for more than 80 years, finally dissolving in the 1930s. During that time, the so-called "Pinkerton men" tirelessly pursued such notorious criminals as Butch Cassidy's Wild Bunch, and they almost always got their man—their failure to catch the James-Younger gang was probably the worst blemish on their reputation. The agency grew so skilled that its methods were used as a model when the U.S. government formed the Federal Bureau of Investigation (FBI) in 1908. Its logo of a watchful eye also gave birth to the modern term "private eye."

Samuel farm at the time. In the years that followed, he would take his alibis a step farther by writing letters to Missouri newspapers defending himself.

The gang's first several robberies were pulled off by Jesse, Frank, Cole Younger, and bushwhackers such as Archie Clement. In 1868, after several of the bushwhackers had been killed by Union lawmen, Cole suggested they recruit two of his teenaged brothers, Jim and Bob. Over the years that followed, dozens of different "fringe" outlaws would ride with this core of cousins.

From 1868 to 1873, the James-Younger gang struck banks in Missouri and Kentucky with increasing daring and violence. In December 1869, Jesse was drawn to a bank in Gallatin, Missouri, by the false rumor that a cashier there was a former Union commander. Jesse entered the bank, drew his pistol, and calmly shot the man twice, killing him.

Even as such deadly raids sparked increasingly massive manhunts, Jesse was becoming a celebrity across the country and a hero locally. Although many people despised the gang's killings, they nonetheless delighted in reading the thrilling newspaper accounts. Many Missourians, still bitter about the Confederacy's defeat, cheered each time the outlaws struck the Yankee monetary system, and did what they could to protect the gang. As newspapers churned out Jesse James stories, so did wildly popular—and largely fictional—pamphlet-sized storybooks called dime novels.

By 1873, banks were no longer such inviting targets for robbery. Many added sophisticated vault locks, and some towns formed volunteer organizations ready to put up a fight at a moment's notice. And not least of the gang's concerns was that the fearsome Pinkerton's National Detective Agency had been hired to put an end to the crime spree. All of this compelled Jesse and his partners to look at a new target: trains.

In the post-war era known as "Reconstruction," the recently built railroads were used to carry money and goods across the country to help with the rebuilding and growth process. To die-hard rebels like Jesse, the trains and railroad officials were yet another long arm of the oppressive North, charging Southern farmers outrageous freight rates and bringing in new Yankee settlers.

The James-Younger gang made its first strike against the railroads on July 21, 1873, near the tiny town of Adair, Iowa. Just before dawn, the gang tore up the rails along a blind curve. The Chicago, Rock Island & Pacific train engine plowed into the earth and crushed the engineer as it tipped over. Masked bandits raided a safe in the mail car and then went through the passenger cars collecting watches, cash, and jewels. Infuriated lawmen hunted in vain as four more trains were hit—and tens of thousands of dollars taken—over the next few years.

In 1874, both Jesse and Frank were married. Jesse wed his cousin Zee Mimms, whom he had fallen in love with nine years earlier as she nursed him to health. Although Zee knew Jesse was a criminal, she loved him deeply and chose to dwell on his quick smile and other positive traits. He rarely drank or smoked, never swore in the presence of women, and was completely devoted to his family.

HOOSAC TUNNEL FOR THE WEST

The James-Younger gang, disenchanted with robbing banks, turned its focus to the expanding railroad system in the early 1870s.

Jesse and Zee would have two children together: a son named Jesse Edward in 1875, and a daughter named Mary in 1879.

In the mid-1870s, perhaps to better keep the law guessing, Jesse and his partners ranged more widely, holding up stagecoaches in Louisiana and Arkansas and banks in Kansas and Mississippi. Pinkerton men—who were tiring of futile chases and angered that three agents had already been killed in pursuit of the gang—decided to stake out the James family home. Zerelda soon saw shadowy figures lurking outside the house day and night.

Things came to a head on the bitterly cold night of January 26, 1875. After spying two sweaty horses in the Samuel barn, Pinkerton agents were sure they had the James boys at last and hurled a 30-pound (13.7 kg) kerosene smoke bomb through the house's living room window. In fact, the only people inside at the time were Zerelda, Reuben, and Archie Samuel, Jesse's eight-year-old stepbrother. The bomb exploded, killing Archie and tearing off Zerelda's right arm below the elbow.

The incident made national headlines, generating vast public sympathy for the James boys. Jesse, for his part, nearly went insane with rage. Although he longed to kill Allan Pinkerton, he soon drew up a different plan for revenge. The plan called for a strike so bold it could not help but be seen as a mockery of the North and its hired guns. He decided he would launch a bank raid in the heart of Yankee country, and he set his sights on the Minnesota town of Northfield.

Running and Gunning

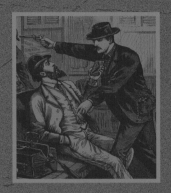

Legend likes to recall Jesse as a daredevil equally expert at handling a charging steed or a pistol. Stories have been told of him taking on Union patrols almost single-handedly, riding into their midst with the reins in his teeth, blazing away with a gun in each hand, then pulling new ones from the small arsenal of Colt pistols tucked into his belt. There certainly is no denying his daring. He was reportedly the first robber to enter a bank and the last to leave, and was a ferocious fighter when cornered. In truth, however, Jesse was not a particularly skilled shooter and exhibited no greater horsemanship than many riders of the time. Of the gang, it is said that Cole Younger was the best gunman and most knowledgeable horseman. What kept Jesse alive more than his skills with a gun were his instincts, almost paranoid watchfulness, and endurance. On several occasions, he was wounded by enemy fire but managed to escape on horseback, riding long distances through incredible pain.

CHAPTER THREE

⚜ The End of the Road ⚜

THE YEAR 1876 WAS AN EVENTFUL ONE IN WILD WEST LORE.
In June, famed Indian fighter

GEORGE ARMSTRONG CUSTER

AND HIS TROOPS WERE SLAUGHTERED BY THOUSANDS OF

Sioux and Cheyenne warriors in Montana.

In August, legendary gunman "Wild Bill" Hickok was

shot in the back in a saloon in South Dakota. As he

rode north with seven companions, 29-year-old

Jesse James was about to add to this eventful history.

The gang pulled into Northfield on September 7 and headed toward the First National Bank, said to be the richest bank west of the Mississippi River. The eight men cut an impressive figure. All rode magnificent horses and wore shiny black boots and long coats called dusters. Northfield's citizens watched with suspicion as the strangers split into three groups, and Jesse and two others entered the bank.

Within moments, Jesse leaped over the counter and put his pistol to the cheek of a cashier named Joseph Heywood. The cashier boldly refused to open the vault, even after taking a punch to the ribs. Outside the bank, when one of the lookouts roughly pushed away a curious citizen, a shout went up: "They're robbing the bank!" Barbers, butchers, and merchants picked up guns and started shooting. Furious to have nothing to show for the 400-mile (640 km) journey, Jesse shot Heywood in the head.

By the time Jesse reached his saddle, two of the robbers—Bill Chadwell and Clel Miller—lay dead in the dirt. Shopkeepers blasted away with shotguns, and other citizens poured down rifle fire from second-story windows. All three Younger brothers were hit. The gang returned fire as best it could, killing one Swedish settler. Church bells rang out as Jesse spurred his horse into an alley, followed closely by Frank, the wounded Youngers, and Charlie Pitts.

The Youngers and Pitts limped south, while Jesse and Frank made for the Dakotas, all the while pursued by huge, relentless posses. Two weeks later, a posse caught the Youngers and shot Pitts to death at a swampy hideout near Madelia, Minnesota. The

This photo, said to have been taken at a cave hideout, depicts Jesse (left) and two unidentified members of his gang.

Bob Ford

B ob Ford was born in Missouri in 1861 and took up horse rustling and petty crimes as a teenager. In early 1882, after two years of living on the outskirts of the James gang, Bob worked his way into Jesse's inner circle and—along with his brother Charley—began cautiously looking for a chance to kill him. "We waited a long time to catch Jesse without his revolvers," Bob later explained, "knowing that unless he put them off we could not fetch him." To his dismay, Bob's slaying of Jesse earned him everlasting scorn. He attempted a brief theatrical career, touring the country in a vaudeville show called *How I Killed Jesse James*, but he was frequently booed offstage. His brother Charley, wracked with chronic illness and fear of reprisal from Frank James, killed himself in 1884. Bob met his end in 1892 after opening a saloon in Colorado. One night Ed Kelly, a cousin of the Youngers, walked in, leveled a shotgun at Bob, and said, "This one's for Jesse" before firing both barrels.

James brothers, shocked by the ferocity of what they had expected to be pushover Yankee hicks, embarked on an exhausting route southward.

Jesse and Frank laid low in Texas for a while and then moved with their families to Tennessee in 1877. For the next two years, they did their best to pass themselves off as regular citizens. Jesse went by the name "J.D. Howard," sang in the church choir, and raced his horse at the county fair. He assumed the guise of a wheat farmer near Nashville but paid his bills with stolen money.

By the end of those two years, however, Jesse was itching to rob again. He was bored, his money was running low, and he longed to return to Missouri. Most importantly, he wanted to continue his personal war and return luster to the name of Jesse James. Since the Northfield disaster, newspapers had suggested that the Yankee town had scared the fight out of him.

The first step in Jesse's comeback was to find new partners. Frank reluctantly agreed to pick up his guns again, but the Youngers were locked away in a Minnesota prison. A gang was soon patched together with various gunmen and horse thieves. Playing lesser roles in the gang were two young newcomers: brothers Charley and Bob Ford.

The new James gang pulled off its first job in October 1879, holding up a train near Glendale, Missouri, and riding off with about $6,000 in cash. Over the next two years, the gang struck several more trains in Missouri, a bank in Alabama, and a stagecoach in Kentucky. Dime novelists again churned out riveting accounts of

This engraving depicts Bob Ford fatally shooting Jesse from behind. The act earned Ford dubious fame and, eventually, a similar death.

Jesse's exploits, and he grew a fashionable beard to better appear the rascal the stories made him out to be.

Headlines notwithstanding, however, things were not going particularly well for the gang. About half a dozen holdups had netted little money, two gang members had been captured, and several civilians had been murdered, including a train conductor shot by Jesse. In early 1881, newly elected Missouri governor Thomas Crittenden announced his determination "to destroy outlawry in this state, whose head and front is the James gang." The governor then convinced railroad officials to help put up a $10,000 reward for the capture of Jesse or Frank James. It was the biggest bounty ever offered for an American outlaw.

Frank saw the writing on the wall before Jesse did. In early 1882, he returned to his Tennessee farm. Shortly thereafter, Jesse moved back to Missouri with his wife and children, renting a small house on a hill above the town of St. Joseph. There he assumed the name "Thomas Howard" and began plotting a bank raid in nearby Platte City, Missouri. Becoming desperate for partners, he contacted the Ford brothers.

Jesse had always harbored some suspicions about Bob, but he could not have known how deep his treachery ran. Hoping to claim fame and the $10,000 reward, the younger Ford met in secret with Governor Crittenden and police officials in a Kansas City, Missouri, hotel. At the meeting, it is believed that Ford promised to pass some of the reward money to the officials in exchange for a pardon for Jesse's murder.

On the morning of April 3, 1882, the Fords had breakfast at Jesse's house, and the three discussed plans for the raid. Jesse had taken off his gun harness in order not to raise suspicion among passersby who might look through the window, and Bob saw his chance. Noticing a picture frame in need of dusting, Jesse stepped onto a chair to clean it. Bob quickly moved behind him and raised his pistol. The last thing Jesse heard was the cock of a gun, and Bob shot him in the back of the head.

At the sound, Zee rushed into the room to find Jesse lying on the floor and the Fords running out the front door. Bob Ford hurried to the telegraph office and sent the governor a simple message: "I've got him sure." The impossible news spread like wildfire throughout St. Joseph and then the nation: the legendary Jesse James was dead.

Three days later, Jesse was buried at the Samuel farmstead, with 2,000 people in attendance. A white marble headstone was soon erected that read: "In loving remembrance, Jesse W. James, aged 34 years, 6 months, 28 days, murdered by a traitor and coward whose name is not worthy to appear here."

A Remorseful Killer?

During the very first bank robbery by the James gang, a college student named George Wymore was shot and killed in Liberty, Missouri, by one of the robbers as the gang left town. Some sources claim that a few days later, the young man's parents received a letter from Jesse and Frank James expressing regret for the "accidental" killing. Whether this is fact or fiction is uncertain, but such anecdotes have fueled the myth that Jesse was more a kind-hearted rogue than a dark-hearted killer. Historians believe Jesse killed at least six men—most of them unarmed—during his life of outlawry, and an untold number as a teenaged guerrilla. There is little to suggest that he truly was bothered by killing; the famous detective Allan Pinkerton once said, "He is utterly devoid of fear and has no more [remorse] about cold-blooded murder than he has about eating his breakfast." Jesse himself once declared, "A man who is a damned enough fool to refuse to open a safe or a vault when he is covered with a pistol ought to die."

CHAPTER FOUR

A Devilish Hero

IN THE DAYS AFTER
JESSE'S DEATH,
a deep reluctance to damn him swept across the country.
Newspapers bid the outlaw farewell
WITH FOND HEADLINES,

and the law relaxed its pursuit of Frank. As Jesse's family

was showered with sympathy, his killer earned his own fame,

but not of the sort he had expected. Scorn was heaped upon

Bob Ford and the devious manner in which he had killed Jesse.

A song was soon written that dubbed him "that dirty little

coward that shot Mr. Howard." No matter where he went

or what he did, he could never escape the "coward" insults.

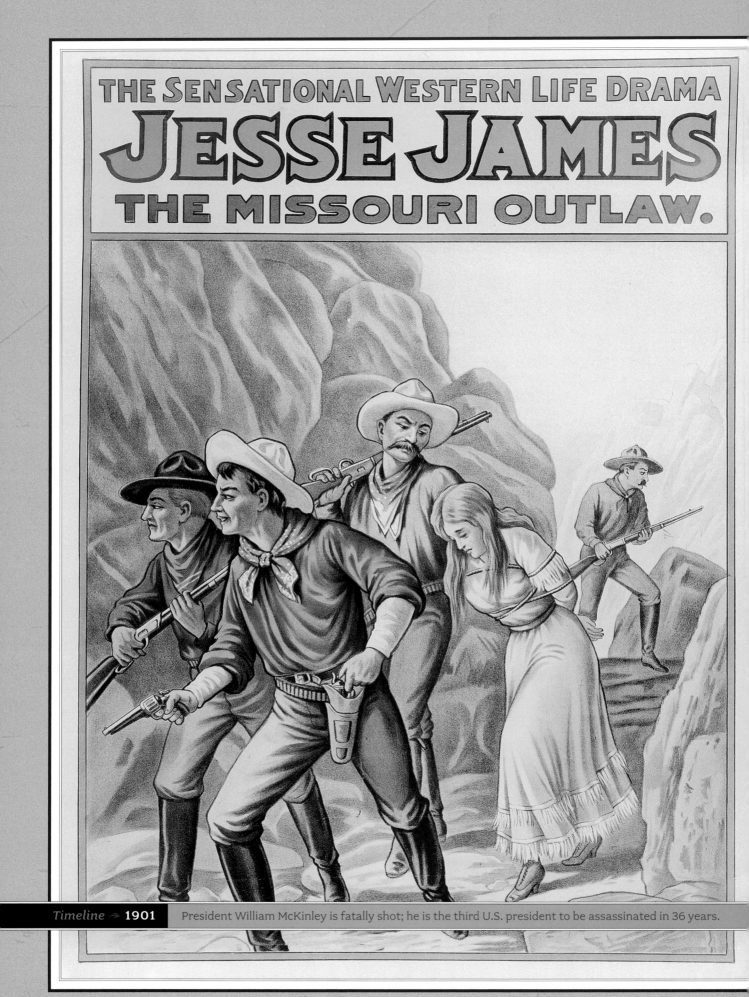

THE *SENSATIONAL* WESTERN LIFE DRAMA
JESSE JAMES
THE MISSOURI OUTLAW.

Timeline ⇒ 1901 President William McKinley is fatally shot; he is the third U.S. president to be assassinated in 36 years.

Many people saw Jesse as a Robin Hood of the Wild West; others regarded him as a cunning but vicious criminal.

Almost immediately after Jesse's murder, his legend grew tremendously. Much of America chose to remember him less as a villain than a wayward son. Stories that portrayed him as clever and kind-hearted—a sort of Robin Hood figure—were repeated often, such as the story of his encounter with the widow of a former bushwhacker. Hiding out at the widow's farmstead, Jesse learned that she was deep in debt and that a greedy banker was coming that afternoon to seize her property. He gave her the $500 she needed and urged her to get a signed receipt. She did, and as the banker left the farm, Jesse's gang met him on the road, reclaimed the money, and rode off with a wave.

The Robin Hood theme earned staying power thanks to songs written shortly after Jesse's death. The most famous was "The Ballad of Jesse James," an overnight sensation written by a minstrel named Billy Gashade. The lyrics ran in newspapers across the country, and the tune became a standard in saloons for years. One of the stanzas went:

> *He robbed from the rich and was a friend to the poor;*
> *He had a heart and a hand and a brain.*
> *With his brother Frank, he robbed the Northfield Bank*
> *And stopped the Glendale train.*

Decades later, two U.S. presidents—Theodore Roosevelt and Harry Truman—offered similar praise. "Jesse James was not actually a bad man at heart," Truman declared while in office. "He stole from the rich and gave to the poor, which, in general, is not

Frank James

Jesse's older brother was born on January 10, 1843. He was named Alexander Franklin James but decided early on that "Alexander" was too sissy-sounding and preferred to be called "Frank." Always called "Mr. Frank" by his mother, Frank was a contemplative man who spoke slowly and enjoyed moments of solitude when he could read the Bible or the works of William Shakespeare. An acquaintance once said of the James boys, "Jesse laughs at everything—Frank at nothing at all." Although he lacked Jesse's fire and charm, Frank was well-liked among his comrades and was said to be able to ride faster and farther than any other member of the James-Younger gang. And even though he frequently quarreled with Jesse over gang decisions, Frank was loyal to his brother and saved his life in more than one shootout. After Jesse's murder, he applied himself to various honest trades, including that of a shoe salesman, horserace starter, and tour guide at the James family farm. He died of a heart attack on February 18, 1915.

a bad policy. I am convinced that Jesse would have been an asset to his community if he had not been diverted into a lawless life."

Frank James helped forge a favorable legacy for his brother as well. After Jesse's funeral, Frank turned himself in for trial. Sympathetic juries acquitted him of virtually all charges, and he spent less than two years in custody. During the trials, Frank's lawyer, a notorious Confederate newspaperman named John Edwards, took advantage of the fondness that still lingered for Jesse. Jesse and Frank were just misunderstood Missouri boys, he argued, driven to a life of crime by Yankee mistreatment and corruption. After his acquittal, Frank became a popular celebrity and earned money by telling his own embellished tales of their lives and deeds.

Although dime novels remained popular—and as fantastical as ever—after Jesse's death, his adventures were no longer portrayed only on printed pages. By the mid-1880s, the exploits of the James gang were being acted out onstage by traveling theater companies. Such performances remained popular until the 1920s, when the advent of motion pictures largely replaced stage productions as popular entertainment.

Dozens of movies have been made about the life and times of Jesse James. Two of the most critically acclaimed were *Jesse James* (1939) and *The Great Northfield, Minnesota Raid* (1972). The films present starkly different takes on Jesse's character. In *Jesse James*, the outlaw is portrayed by actor Tyrone Power as a wholesome farm boy pushed to criminal deeds by brutal railroad men who kill his mother and terrorize Missouri farmers. As he robs railroad passengers, he politely thanks them and refuses to take jewelry from women.

In *The Great Northfield, Minnesota Raid*, on the other hand, Jesse is portrayed by actor Robert Duvall as an egotistical, psychotic killer. Even as two of his fellow gang members lie in Northfield coffins, he reflects with glee on the way the mere mention of his name caused a bank teller to faint. The film portrays Jesse as a criminal so vile he kills an old widow for her raincoat and umbrella.

It was not only movies that kept Jesse in the public eye in the 20th century, however. He made the news periodically in the early 1900s as a number of old men announced themselves to be the real Jesse James, claiming to have faked their death in 1882 in order to escape the law. Although the claims were met with great skepticism, conspiracy theorists managed to keep the rumors alive for years. In 1995, to put the issue to rest once and for all, Jesse's grave in Kearney was exhumed, and DNA tests were performed. The tests revealed a 99.7 percent probability that the grave did in fact hold Jesse's remains. Several years later, the gun that put Jesse in the ground made news as well. In 2003, the Smith & Wesson revolver used by Bob Ford was sold at auction for $350,000.

Just as towns robbed by Jesse during his heyday proudly staked their claim in American lore, a number of places today continue to promote their close ties to the legendary outlaw. There are several museums devoted to Jesse, including the Jesse James Farm and Museum in Kearney; the Jesse James Home and Patee House Museum in St. Joseph, Missouri; and the Jesse James Museum in

Tyrone Power (left) and Henry Fonda (right) portrayed the James brothers in the popular 1939 film Jesse James.

Wichita, Kansas. Another town forever linked to Jesse is North-field, Minnesota, the site of his greatest defeat. Northfield commemorates the infamous raid gone wrong every September with the "Defeat of Jesse James Days," a four-day festival complete with a reenactment of that fateful day in 1876.

More than 120 years after his death, Jesse James is still remembered as the ultimate outlaw, the uncatchable rebel. For 16 years, he fought what some considered an unjust system of authority. And for the most part, against all odds, he won. Some say he was just a product of his times, a hard man forged by the fires of war. To others he was a cold-blooded killer who used his hatred of all things Yankee as an excuse to commit murder and fill his pockets. Robin Hood or devil on horseback? The questions—and the story—will linger forever in American mythology.

No Rest for the Wicked

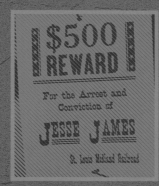

Thanks in part to the grossly exaggerated tales of the dime novels published in the 1870s and 1880s, as well as the word-of-mouth legends that followed his death, Jesse's life is frequently regarded as one of celebrity adventure. That he was a celebrity is beyond dispute. During his day, he was as famous as the president of the United States. Yet for all of the headlines he created, Jesse's life was one of unrelieved danger and little rest. He was constantly hunted, saw many of his friends die violently, and had cause to watch his back even among his partners. His life of crime dictated that he flee from hideout to hideout across several states, sleep lightly, and be heavily armed at all times. It is likely his emotions were mirrored in comments Frank James made after surrendering for trial in 1882: "I am tired of this life of taut nerves, of night-riding and day-hiding, of constant listening for footfalls, cracking twigs, and rustling leaves and creaking doors; tired of seeing Judas on the face of every friend I know...."

Further Information

BOOKS

Brant, Marley. *Outlaws: The Illustrated History of the James-Younger Gang*. Montgomery, Ala.: Black Belt Press, 1997.

Bruns, Roger A. *Jesse James: Legendary Outlaw*. Berkeley Heights, N.J.: Enslow Publishers, 1998.

Wukovits, John F. *Jesse James*. New York: Chelsea House Publications, 2002.

FILMS

The Great Northfield, Minnesota Raid. 1972. 91 min. Universal Pictures.

In Search of Jesse James. 2001. 46 min. A&E Entertainment.

Jesse James. 1939. 106 min. Twentieth Century Fox.

WEB SITES

The James-Younger Gang Homepage
http://www.islandnet.com/~the-gang/index.html

Jesse James: Folklore Hero or Cold-Blooded Killer?
http://www.legendsofamerica.com/WE-JesseJames.html

Jesse James: Riding Hell-Bent for Leather into Legend
http://www.crimelibrary.com/americana/jesse

Index